HEALING, HARMONY & HEALTH

Barney Camfield

BOSSINEY BOOKS

First published in 1985
by Bossiney Books,
St Teath, Bodmin, Cornwall.
Typeset, printed and bound in Great Britain
by A. Wheaton & Co., Exeter.

Plate Acknowledgments
Front cover by Mark Bygrave
Back cover by Vic Fowler
Ray Bishop: pages 5, 40, 76, 88
Mary Lou North: pages 16, 17,34
Alice Boyd: pages 9, 32
Paul Honeywill: pages 25, 44, 47
Wendy Selby: pages 18, 19
Woolf-Greenham Collection: page 77
Julia Davey: page 11
Richard Isbell: page 15
Bryan Russell: page 63
The posters have been reproduced by
kind permission of Argus Communications UK,
Harlow, England.

ISBN 0 948158 01 8

Contents

About the Author and the Book

Barney (christened Bernard Jesse Oliver) Camfield was born at Barters Farm, eight miles south of Salisbury and has always retained a love of farming and country life.

After service in the commandos during the second world war, he was invalided out in 1945 and became involved in earning his living in films and television. After a study of psychology, though, this has been his primary interest and he has become well-known for his work in the field of psychosomatic medicine and 'healing'.

Mr Camfield has been minister of Moretonhampstead Unitarian Church since 1967, is Westcountry Chairman of the National Federation of Spiritual Healers and founded the Moreton Healing Fellowship with branches in the South and West.

He is perhaps best known for his work in 'psycho-expansion', a method of psychological self-discovery.

Though known to many people in the Westcountry through his radio broadcasts and appearances on TV, here Barney Camfield makes his debut as a Bossiney author. In *Healing, Harmony and Health* he explores healing in its various forms, the significance of handwriting and dreams, and psycho-expansion. This is a book which offers help and hope to many. As the author reflects: '. . . if we change our ideas from fear and competitiveness to co-operation and expansive out-going loving kindness . . . we benefit by gaining in confidence and understanding . . .'

Author, Barney Camfield.

Chapter 1

What is a 'Healer'?

How are you? I'm fine thanks!

Apart from crushing my left foot between two ships, and having a hole put through my chest by the Waffen SS. Plus a fractured skull, broken neck, broken ribs, crushed right leg. Oh, yes; and depression, shingles, diverticulosis/itis, pancreatitis, angina and a few little things like jaundice, bronchitis and the usual plethora of childhood ailments. Apart from the aforementioned, I've kept remarkably fit.

And I've spent — mostly during war time — about two years hospitalised in twenty four different hospitals. In over sixty years I've been treated by physicians, consultants, surgeons, osteopaths, chiropractors, healers, physiotherapists, etc.

All of the above therapists can be described quite correctly as 'healers'. But the term 'healer' is commonly used to describe those who heal by the 'laying on of hands'.

Not that it is strictly accurate as the healing practitioner will only too readily admit. He — or she — says that a healer is but a channel of healing energy. And he/she feels, too, that the healing energy does not just come *from* him but rather *through* him. That's not necessarily simply a theory; it *feels* that way. The patient appears to draw through the healer a collection or blend of energies, some of which can be measured, which assists the body of the sufferer in some way or other to correct the physical or mental problem.

I can't remember when or who, but I recall hearing of a surgeon who said that a surgeon can cut and sew, medicinal treatment and

A youngish, beardless (and slim) Barney Camfield telling the story of negro spirituals and jazz with musical illustrations by Rod Mason's Jass Band. Westward TV's announcer Stuart Hutchison on drums.

nursing can be given, but the body has then to heal itself. Our own 'life force' takes over and completes the job.

But what is that 'life force'? Some healers speak of etheric energies and, while science may well be on the verge of discovering the nature of some of them, they haven't done so yet. Infra red and ultra violet can be measured emanating from the hands of a healer and increasing up to a thousand times more than the usual minimal amount present.

That doesn't happen, though, when it is not needed. Often I have been asked by someone – including reporters – to put my hands on them because they have been told that my hands have been 'red hot' or someone has felt a tingling or a pulling sensation. I ask them if they have anything wrong and if they say that they have not then I tell them that they are not liable to feel anything. Only when there is a need, it seems, are the healing energies drawn through. And it's not my hands which are hot. The energies involved heat the patient's body.

It seems, too, that there are many and various sensations and reactions experienced by patients, some of which just cannot be described. Time also plays a part; the particular physical problem indicates that some kind of a pattern exists. For example, I try to make sure that anyone suffering from a blocked sinus does not leave until half an hour after treatment has finished. I have found that if patients drive off directly after treatment they often have to stop their cars to deal with a flood of mucus! This tends to start twenty minutes after treatment has finished.

Those with a hearing problem may experience heat inside the ear during treatment, but very little increase in hearing. Later, they comment: 'I left you in Plymouth and while driving through Truro realised that I was hearing much more clearly.' There appears to be about an hour's delay in the effect when treating most hearing problems.

That's the rule but there are exceptions which test this rule; probably depending upon exactly what is wrong. It must be made clear, too, that in the vast majority of cases the benefits are temporary. That is they do not last after just one treatment but that several – or even many – treatments are necessary before there is

Harmony in the countryside.

a sustained improvement. I have experienced, however, a number of 'one off' cases where the benefit has lasted after just one treatment.

In a number of cases where there is a displacement of some kind, say in the spine or a joint, the correction time can vary. I have been told by patients, for example, 'Two hours after I left you I felt a movement in my back, there was a click and it went back in place!' Sometimes the move can take place next day, within half an hour or perhaps even minutes after treatment.

I remember one sixteen-year-old girl, over six feet tall, who had been brought along by her mother. I was told that she had had repeated treatments from an osteopath or chiropractor, who succeeded each time in putting her spine back in place, but that it was painful and she had come to dread these sessions. They had been told of me by someone who had benefited by my 'laying on of hands' — I do not manipulate at all — and felt that perhaps there would be a gentler and more lasting effect.

I gave her treatment; she could feel a 'pulling' in her spine and a certain amount of heat. She changed places with her mother who was also in need of help for a physical condition, and I had been working for about ten minutes when the girl gave a yelp and said that her back was all right now and that the ache had gone. But the pain when the back had righted itself was as bad as when she had been manipulated by the osteopath.

Where there is a displacement with resulting pain and ache, there is usually an intensification of the pain during treatment but the area lessens and the pain seems to come to a definable point. It appears that the healing energy continues to work for some time, even after treatment has ceased. Again, it may take a number of treatments to correct the problem.

The character of the patient has a part to play, too, but I want to deal with that at greater length later.

Arthritis in its various forms is something which is crippling and exceedingly painful. Many and varied, too, are the treatments but so many of those suffering from arthritis, who come to our clinics for treatment, have been previously helped primarily by pain killers

Some people claim to find great healing energy from trees.

This little chap receiving healing treatment was once critically ill. Now he's almost hyperactive!

of one sort or another. I make sure that these patients are told – and given written material – explaining that, while they usually experience great relief during the treatment, within twelve or twenty-four hours the pain is back with a vengeance with perhaps a slight improvement after that. They may say while having treatment that it is 'wonderfully soothing' or 'comforting' but there is an inclination next day to say that they wished they had never met me.

One such case comes to mind in connection with a television programme I had been asked to take part in. Dr Alec Forbes had asked me to give healing to a patient while linked to a battery powered electro-encephalograph. The patient would also be connected to a separate machine, both of which would show our individual brainwaves. Healers are supposed to have a strong 'alpha' wave and also experiments have shown that when healing is given the patient's brainwaves tend to change and match the healer's pattern of waves.

I asked the producer of the programme if they could find the patient themselves, preferably someone who had never received healing treatment from me or anyone else. I did not want it thought that there had been any kind of influence. They apparently got in touch with the Arthritis & Rheumatism Council and a volunteer, Norah, appeared at the studio shortly before the programme was due to be taped.

Geoffrey Blundell arrived from London with his two machines, much too late for there to be any trial of the machines. In fact, they were still being set up after the start of the show during the running of a film. But the demonstration worked. Yes, my 'alpha' rhythm was strong. And it and the other brain rhythms were quite different from those of the patient. I stood behind her and gave her healing and within a couple of minutes her brainwaves changed and began to match mine. Upon being questioned, she said that she felt a lovely comfortable glow!

I had warned her that she would most probably feel extra pain the following day. But what I hadn't thought about too much was just how long the period of healing was going to be! I don't give arthritics too long on the first run because I don't want the patient to suffer too much. I try to get them used to it slowly. But on this occasion we couldn't move while Alec Forbes, the interviewer and Geoffrey Blundell were discussing healing and brainwaves, the machines and goodness knows what. And I couldn't turn it off! The healing I mean.

Poor Norah. She told me later that week that the following day she was in such pain that she spent the day in bed. And she wished then that she had never met me! But the following day she felt fine. No arthritic pain; and she hasn't suffered from it since she told me. And that was six years ago. She comes now to most Saturday afternoon sessions, where we hold a short service followed by healing and tea and biscuits.

Chapter 2

How graphology can help you find problems you didn't know you had!

I was talking at a seminar in a Midland town and was explaining that we often habitually think in 'figures of speech' and even voice these thoughts aloud. As a result we instruct our bodies to behave accordingly. One example I gave was of patients who suffer from nausea and vomiting, sometimes for years, without benefiting from medical treatment. As a last resort they come to me as a healer.

I explained that it would depend upon my judgment of the patient's ability to accept the implications of the following question and how often they could visit me in the next few weeks as to how soon I would ask them, 'Do you ever think or ever say: "He makes me sick", "You make me sick", "It makes me sick" or something on those lines?' And I said, if there was a partner, a husband or wife, with the patient, the partner would perhaps make an immediate response and say that this was so. But often with very little thought, the patient would agree that indeed he did use this phrase quite frequently. 'Perhaps you don't realise it', I would say, 'but what you are doing is to *instruct* your body to *feel* sick!'

As I reached this point at the seminar, I saw a lady in the front row grow quite pale. She was one of several who afterwards told me that I had hit the nail on the head. For two years, she said, she had been suffering from nausea and vomiting. Medical examinations, barium meals and treatment followed but it all seemed to have little effect. 'I realise now', she said, 'what the trouble is. I've got twin boys aged eighteen. They've had motorbikes since they were sixteen and I'm always screaming, "You two make me sick! You don't take any care!" She paused, 'Now I know why I feel as I do.'

Mind you, at that seminar I also had people who dismissed the idea. Seldom do I get away without disagreement and, primarily because I would rather spend my time on giving treatment rather than on research — although I'm always willing to co-operate in that field — and because I don't keep detailed records, again due to demands upon my time, I can only give anecdotal evidence from over thirty years work in the field.

But before I give you more examples of the links between thought, emotion and our physical problems, I want to talk about handwriting and dreams. Yes, there is a connection as you will see.

Graphology, or the study of handwriting, can give important clues as to the character and the mood of the writer of a letter. And it isn't mysterious. It is an art and a science, perhaps, but it is based upon commonsense and observation.

Take, for instance, the shape of the writing. If it slopes upwards from left to right, then you can take it that the writer is optimistic — at the time of writing. Perhaps connected with what he is writing about, but not necessarily. Anyway, he is telling you that to him 'things are looking up'!

If the handwriting slopes down from left to right, pessimism is shown, perhaps depression. I remember, in 1954, when I was assisting a solicitor with psychological advice in connection with

A Dumnonian Rock of Ages on Dartmoor.

573
6
11

Stop talking and say something! The author (left) at the Unitarian Church at Moretonhampstead.
Below left: 'We miss these two little helpers now they are in Hong Kong.'
Below: Serving refreshment after the afternoon service.

one of his clients, I received a letter from him which had been addressed by hand. I was immediately struck by the slope of the handwriting, which to me indicated that the writer was practically suicidal. I 'phoned him and told him my thoughts and he said he would find out who had addressed the envelope and come back to me.

The writer was a teenager who had been assisting with clerical work for several years. He was badly crippled, could walk only with assistance and then with great difficulty. His distorted body also meant that he had to have a great deal of help in many other ways, too. His greatest help throughout his life had been his mother. My solicitor friend told me that his mother had died three days before. No wonder his sadness, his depression showed as it did.

Have you ever seen a letter with no margins? With writing from edge to edge — even perhaps with a few lines written upside down between the lines! Well, it saves using another sheet of paper doesn't it? And that's just what such a writer believes, feels, must be done. He must be careful, not wasteful. It may be because he is really in need or it maybe that, while comfortably off, he's going to see that he remains that way by not being wasteful! Again, an indication of a belief, a mood, perhaps. An indication of character; because our character is the sum of our beliefs, our conclusions.

Some make a habit of starting words with the first letter separate, while the rest of the letters in the word are joined. This indicates a person who stops to think before he starts anything. While some join the letters of a word leaving the last letter separated, indicating that the writers get moving with some idea or other and hesitate towards the end, wondering if what they set out to do was quite

Figure 1

crossbar flying away to right — impetuosity

crossbar not reaching beyond vertical stroke — hesitancy

crossbar high — dominating

crossbar low — under pressure

Figure 2

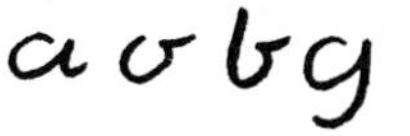

gaps in rounded letters — open minded, perhaps gullible. Can't keep secrets.

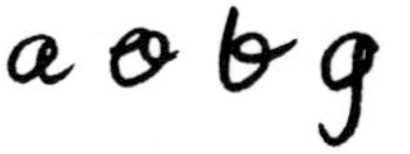

tightly closed, rounded letters — says no more than is necessary, secretive.

flattened bottoms — want to settle down.

such a good idea after all. Commonsense, isn't it? Now you figure out why I often leave both the first and the last letters separate!

If all the letters in most words are joined up, here we find a person who relies upon logic. If practically every letter is separated, then we have someone who is just the opposite; who is continually following ideas which spring to mind, many of which appear quite illogical to others. Not usually a down-to-earth, practical person.

If there is a good balance between joined letters with some letters separated, here we have someone who is logical but knows when to rely on intuition.

With the letter 't' the symbolism is quite obvious. Let's look at *figure 1.* Where the horizontal stroke flies away to the right, here is

Figure 3

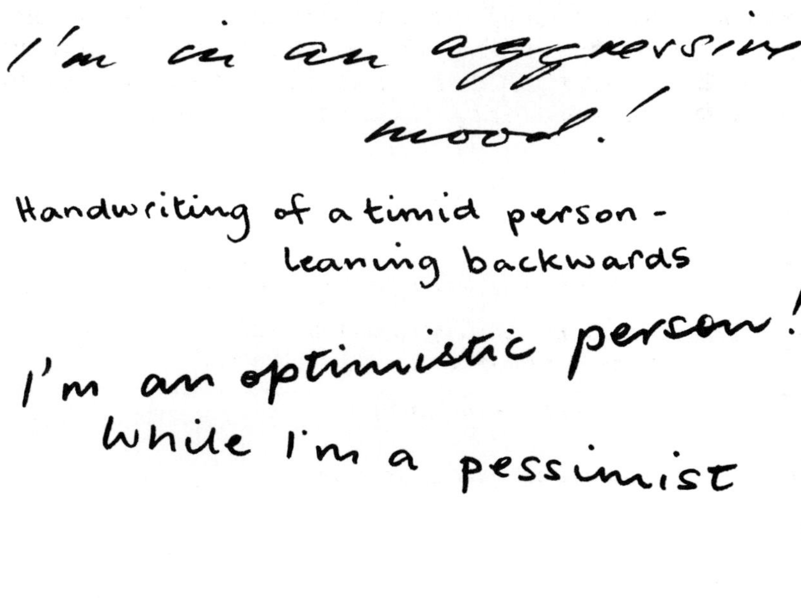

Please don't
tell me
to relax –
it's only
my tension
that's holding
me together.

someone who is a little too impetuous to be always as careful as perhaps he should be. When it doesn't quite reach the vertical stroke, here is a hesitant person, somewhat unsure of himself. Where the horizontal is above or high, you have a strong, perhaps a dominating personality, and where the stroke is low, you have someone under pressure.

Do you write your 'a' or your 'o' or your 'b' or your 'g' with a gap *(figure 2)*? Then you are open-minded – even perhaps gullible – and unlikely to keep secrets! But if they're tightly closed, then you don't give away any more information than you have to.

Most people write with a slight forward slope to their handwriting, showing that they can cope in a fairly relaxed way with life *(figure 3)*. If the handwriting has a pronounced forward slope, then it indicates that the writer has problems which he finds difficult to cope with and he tends to blame others and is aggressive.

If the handwriting leans over backwards, then here we have someone who again has problems which he finds difficulty in coping with but, instead of over compensating as does the forward-sloping, attacking writer, he under compensates, is timid and 'leans over backwards' in order not to provoke others and cause yet more problems. Note the 'figure of speech' there: 'leans over backwards'. Do you see the symbolism in these few graphological examples? They are but a few, so don't jump to too many conclusions when you next get a letter from a friend.

I must admit though that I have had to smile when, for example, I have had a letter where the writer has said that they are so glad that such and such has happened, *but* the slope of the line goes down showing me that the feeling is really the opposite. Or they have said that they are so sorry to hear that this, that and the other has occurred – and the lines are rising!

Now what would you make of a 't' with twists in the crossbar. Well, you've no doubt heard plenty of funny stories and have possibly told a few. In every joke the laugh comes when the unexpected happens, where the 'twist' appears. And that's what you would find with someone who crosses his 't' with a twist. He's a joker – and probably a mimic, too. Easy to see now – and it's only commonsense.

What has this to do with sickness and healing? I'll tell you, but first I want to say something about dreams.

Barney Camfield greeting Plymouth's Lord Mayor at the first ever Mayoral visit to Westward TV's studio in 1962.

Chapter 3

Dreams can give you clues to your problems and how to solve them.

Practically everyone admits to dreaming at some time or other. A few say that they have never dreamt. However, many tests have been made on both dreamers and non-dreamers at neurological clinics. These tests include such electronic equipment as electro-encephalographs which measure brainwaves. In both dreamers and non-dreamers, brainwave patterns have shown changes of a similar nature, together with typical signs of dreaming such as rapid eye movements.

It seems that everyone dreams but that not everyone can remember their dreams. Remember when you have had a dream which you *knew* was interesting but: 'It's gone! Can't remember a thing about it!' This can happen within a short time of awakening and getting ready for the day's surprises. It is perhaps because the dream hasn't been thought about, hasn't been introduced properly to the consciousness. If we turn our mind quickly when we become conscious to other matters, the dream disappears rapidly and we cannot recall it easily, if at all. I have, however, known people who have either forgotten a dream – or say that they do not have them – able to recall them during regression.

Dreams are 'out pictures' of our emotions. They tell us how we feel about our problem. Indeed, they are telling us that we do have problems which we have not yet solved; perhaps not only have we not solved them but we are even trying to escape from dealing with them.

Nowadays we can express a good many abstract concepts quite easily. But once upon a time, in the not so far distant past, we did not have this same ability, so we would paint a little word picture. Of friend Jack today we could say, 'He's a religious man', or 'He is a spiritual man'. The listener to our observation would then form an understanding of Jack based upon his own concept of 'religious' and 'spiritual'. Now go back a few thousand years and we would use the kind of language which is found in the authorised version of the Bible, 'Jack walked with the Lord' or 'He dwells in the house of the Lord'.

We can, and still do, paint these word pictures and call them figures of speech, and dreams use this language together with plays on words and other symbolism. They put our emotions into primarily pictorial form; visual because sight is perhaps the most all-embracing of our senses. Dreams are like political cartoons, with a picture which is obvious to us but which has a disguised meaning. That, too, becomes obvious when we realise it is saying, 'It's as if . . .' And that's what our dreams do; they say, 'It is as if . . .' And perhaps you will have two or three dreams, apparently very different but when looked into they say, 'It is as if . . .' 'Or to put it another way . . .' 'Or try this . . .'

Let me give you some examples. We had finished an evening of 'dream work' where we had discussed the dreams of the group present, when one lady said to me, 'I had a dream last night, but in spite of the work we've done over the past few weeks, I just could not find any figures of speech or play on words or any association of ideas. Can't think what it means. It was short and simple: I dreamt that I saw my husband fall out of a window and I had to climb down a ladder and help him back up.'

After discussing the matter for a while, she did indeed find that there were two figures of speech, 'fall out' and 'climb down'. She realised then what her problem was and how it was pictured in the dream. Her husband had 'fallen out' with her the previous day and she said, 'If I don't apologise — whether I'm right or whether I'm wrong — he won't speak to me for three or four days. I can't stand that silence so I always "climb down".' But the fact that she always had to give in annoyed her. She always lost and, as she didn't know what to do about it, she repressed it, but the dream expressed it.

She had been doing dream work with us for some time but could not recognise the clues in this one. It was a problem which would at some time or other have to be dealt with or she could have greater problems to follow. She would either have to accept — as distinct

'I dreamt that I saw my husband fall out of a window . . .'

from 'putting up with' – the situation or go through that which she 'couldn't stand' in order to beat her own repression. Did you note the two figures of speech I put in inverted commas? Often used in dreams!

I would like to stress that it is most important that the dreamer finds the analysis acceptable. The analyst or therapist may have an idea about it but he can only help the dreamer understand. It is the dreamer's dream and her or his opinion matters more than the opinion of the analyst. It is no good the analyst getting frustrated if he sees that, for one reason or another, the dreamer will not accept what to the analyst is so obvious. There is a reason the dreamer *can't* at that time accept what may possibly be true and blocks it out, and if the analyst gets frustrated, *he's* got a problem!

I was giving a talk on dreams to a group of about seventy people when one girl said that she had heard a radio broadcast of mine, a two-hour 'phone-in, on dreams, but daren't 'phone in a dream of hers which intrigued her because it was so stupid! Well, dreams often are, aren't they? She did relate it, however, and she said, 'I was watching with my right eye myself giving birth to a baby from my right ear.' As you can imagine, she got a laugh from the rest of the audience. I asked her how she felt after the dream and she said, 'Relieved.' I ask how people feel about dreams because dreams are concerned with emotions, the movement of feelings.

I then asked her if she had been considering a new venture of any kind at that time and she said that she had. She and a friend had been preparing to start an outside catering business. 'How did it go?' I asked. 'Very well,' she answered. 'Much better than we expected.' Well, we discovered that her dream used both a figure of speech and a play on words. We agreed that one often spoke of a responsibility as a 'baby': 'That's nothing to do with you, that's my baby' or 'I don't want anything to do with that – that's *your* baby!'

And here was a 'new baby' – a new responsibility. Remember that she felt relieved after her dream? Well, I said that I thought her dream was telling her not to worry; that she had the 'right idea' – the 'right-eyed-ear'! Geddit? She specifically mentioned that she was watching, with her right eye, her right ear.

I remember during a later radio programme someone had dreamt that he had a coloured baby in his lap. That's all. Nothing happened. He just had a coloured baby in his lap. I asked what colour. 'Black – and, come to think of it, the head was blacker than

They can because they think they can.

VIRGIL

the rest of the body. The head was quite large, too.' We talk of a 'black outlook'. I've found that quite frequently in dreams something black — often a black or a dark or swarthy person — is some aspect of the dreamer which is concerned with a 'black outlook'. Something about themselves about which they are afraid.

Here the head was emphasised and we often say about something we don't want to have to cope with and haven't asked for as having it 'dumped into my lap'. Baby — responsibility; black — pessimistic outlook about this responsibility; lap — no choice about having to cope with it. Then the dreamer admitted that indeed something like this had occurred. He was an executive in a company and had suddenly been switched to an entirely unfamiliar department about which he knew next to nothing. It had been more or less made clear to him that it was this or being made redundant. He had been briefed verbally but found great difficulty in remembering the workings of this department. Hence the emphasis on the head of the baby. It seemed, too, that he felt that his superiors did not like him and *wanted* him to fail. These were his feelings, based upon his beliefs about the situation. What he needed to do was take a good, long, objective view of the situation to see, if he could, just how his feelings and his beliefs related to the truth. He told me later that he had left the company.

I remember some years ago a girl came to me because she was worried about her imminent marriage. She loved her fiancé, wanted to marry him, but – he did this, he did that and, altogether, his behaviour was such that she was afraid that he would make neither a good husband nor a good father. The more she talked about him, the more angry she became about his behaviour and the more worried she was about the marriage. We talked for a while and booked another appointment for a week's time. I asked her to 'look into' her own attitude towards marriage and to jot down any dreams and bring them along.

One dream she felt strongly about. She was travelling in a vehicle along a road she frequently travelled. She had often passed a house in which she knew lived a black woman, who did not look after her children nor keep the house tidy and clean. On this occasion the vehicle stopped outside the house. She knocked at the door, was greeted by the black woman and invited in. She discovered that the house was spick and span and the children well looked after and happy. She continued her journey. I asked her how she felt and it transpired that she was relieved that the woman wasn't 'as black as she had been painted'.

After about an hour's discussion, she decided that the vehicle represented her progress on 'the road' to marriage, and she realised that before she stopped the road was somewhat bumpy. A house or a room represents an aspect of the self about which one is concerned at the time, and she felt that this house represented marriage and motherhood. Her own mother, she said, was not a good wife or mother and she was afraid that she would follow in her mother's footsteps and be a bad wife and mother, which was a 'black outlook'. But, having 'looked into' the situation – she had done this literally in the dream – she discovered that the truth was not as she had feared. She could be a good wife and mother and, having discussed the matter, she could see plenty of evidence of the differences between her mother and herself, and her fears disappeared.

I asked her how she felt about her fiancé and she replied to the effect that perhaps she had been making too much of things and that he was not a bad fellow at all really! In fact, what she had been doing was to project her fears of her own shortcomings upon her fiancé. And we all do that; project upon others and become angry with them concerning factors which are closely linked to fears about ourselves, which we are afraid to face up to in case they prove to be true. So often, as in the example given, we judge ourselves — and others in consequence — far too harshly. We have to start loving ourselves a lot more, then we find it much easier to love others. Try it some time.

But back to figures of speech and plays on words. I have mentioned that we do dream workshops. We also use dreams in some of our relaxation and psycho-expansion groups. Under these

During the early 1960s. Barney Camfield (left), Bridget Meredith, Westward TV Hostess (centre) and Jessica Camfield (right) judge the Barbican Beauty Queen contest. The winner is on the table.

circumstances I get everyone to think of a problem they have, then relax them and let them have a short dream. It works for a good many people, partially for some and not at all for others.

What must be realised here is that we do not often define our problems; we just worry away, feeling anxious and perhaps depressed. If we talk about our problem to another, then we do to a degree define the problem by putting it into words, by verbalising. But — we do not always tell the complete story to another person. Perhaps there is something that we keep back because we are somewhat ashamed. Sometimes we cannot even admit to ourselves some factors. We just could not mentally cope with knowing the truth about ourselves — we think! Dreams can help by disguising and yet at the same time giving us enough clues to allow the truth to dawn upon us without *too* much of a shock.

Here is an example. After a five minute relaxation dream one man said, 'I dreamt of a monk in a brown habit which was flapping about. He "free-wheeled" downhill and disappeared into a lake. I knew it was in Scotland because I knew the name of the lake was Loch Affeen.' He paused and then said, 'The monk was me. The "brown habit" is drinking too much coffee — it makes me nervous and I get into a terrible "flap". I know it's of my own free will ("free wheel") and I know the problem will disappear, my stress will disappear if I drink something with low caffeine (Loch Affeen).' He tried going without coffee and stuck it for about three days, if I remember rightly, but his intuition did, through the dream, define his problem and give him an answer. One thing he did not mention, nor did I mention it to him, but it was significant. He saw himself as a monk. I'll say no more but think about it. I am sure, though, that you can see the collection of figures of speech and the play on words.

I could say a lot more about dreams; and yes, some people do seem to 'dream true' and see the future but I do not want to go into that aspect at this juncture.

Chapter 4

How your particular physical problem can pinpoint your emotional problem.

The symbolism in handwriting and in dreams is generally accepted in the field of psychology. From these symbols, figures of speech and plays on words, the psychologist can get a very good idea of the character and the problems, frustrations, beliefs and ideas of a person. Now, do you remember what I said in an earlier chapter about my experience over the years that those who came to see me who felt physically 'sick' also had some problem in their life, some aspect of their life – usually connected with another person – which made them 'sick'? During more than thirty years work as a psychotherapist, I have found that there are other physical problems which, when connected with a figure of speech, give me clues to the frustrations which have helped to cause them.

If we are in a state of relaxation, then life energy can flow freely through our body. If we have a problem, we tense up and, somewhere or other, slow up or block this flow of energy. If anyone comes to me with a shoulder problem, then it does not usually take more than a few visits to determine just where lies the frustration connected with 'shouldering responsibility'.

You will have noted that a baby in a dream, usually denotes a problem with responsibility, but occasionally in a dream a shoulder is featured. In physical illness shoulder problems are connected with worry about responsibility. What is more, if the left shoulder is affected, we find that a person has responsibility he does not want but cannot get rid of, while if it is the right shoulder there is some responsibility which he wishes to shoulder but is frustrated in doing so.

Most of us have legs. They are to do with 'going' or 'making progress' or standing still. And I have found that leg troubles give me a clue to the frustration factor in connection with 'making progress'. If the left leg is affected in some way then it tells me that the sufferer is 'going in the wrong direction' or is stuck and unable to make progress. Perhaps he does not know which path is the right one or does not have his mind on it. Usually the hip or the upper part of the leg is affected. Interestingly the ankle or foot is sometimes concerned with one's 'understanding'.

If the right leg is affected then he has his mind on where he wants to get but he can't make the progress he would like to. This can be *physical* movement from one place to another but it is just as likely to be connected with, say, progress in marriage, in his work or his studies or in any other way in which we may speak of progress.

Let me tell you a true story. Just over thirty years ago, a friend asked me if I would be good enough to meet a friend of his who had recently returned from Australia, where he had been involved in treating and researching a particular form of blindness peculiar to the aborigines. He had apparently heard of a paper of mine

'If we are in a state of relaxation then life energy can flow freely through our body . . .'

concerning the psychosomatic factor in cancer. 'Psychosomatics' is the study of mind-body relationships – psyche = mind, soma = body.

My wife and I met him at our mutual friend's house for tea and, at one point, I started to give forth using some shoulder problems as examples. I told him of a patient who had failed time and time again to hold down a job, eventually giving up even bothering to do anything. He had become very withdrawn. After a few sessions, he had begun to realise I think that the only real failure is to give up trying. If you expect to fail, then the simplest way is to make no effort. At the third session it was obvious that he was in pain. His head was to one side – over to the right – and he told me that he had a huge carbuncle on his right shoulder. This told me that he was attempting to shoulder responsibility but found it so difficult that he felt he could explode. He had a 'volcano' on his right shoulder!

This demonstrates the method whereby our emotions and our bodies co-operate to get us out of a tight spot! He knew he *ought* to be more responsible and that he *ought* to keep trying but his fear of failure gave him another way out. Crippled as he was and being in such pain prevented him doing anything.

And I told my new friend of a woman I had met in the street a week or so before. A few months previously I had had several sessions with her and with her husband. She was now suffering from a painful carbuncle on her left shoulder, which also gave her a great deal of pain in the left side of her neck. I quickly repressed a slight smile but she had seen it and said, 'Come on then. Tell me what it means.' 'Well,' I said, 'it could possibly be that you are shouldering responsibility which you don't want but can't get rid of. And perhaps it is connected with someone you may possibly consider to be "a pain in the neck".' Then off she went – 'Well, you know what he's like! I've got to do everything myself and if I say anything to him it makes it worse . . .' After five minutes of letting off steam, her shoulder had relaxed somewhat and she seemed to have forgotten how much pain there had been a short while before.

Our new friend broke in at that point: 'You're not going to tell me that emotions can cause such things as carbuncles,' he said. 'I had a carbuncle on my left hip while I was in Australia and I know that that was through eating bad food.'

'Hold it,' I said, 'why didn't the poison manifest as a carbuncle on your face or as a stomach upset or in some other way? I would say that a carbuncle on your left hip resulted from your feeling of frustration, which made you feel like exploding because you were either not making progress in your work or perhaps you were literally stuck in the outback. Your left leg being symbolic of lack of "progress" or "going in the wrong direction".'

Below: Healing at Moretonhampstead Unitarian Church. Could one call it 'a blessing'?
Right: The basic outlook of the Unitarian Church.

This church welcomes all who seek the meaning of life

It has a respect for Christian tradition coupled with a modern religious outlook which encourages freedom of individual thought

It welcomes all who believe that religion is wider than any one sect and deeper than any one set of opinions

It seeks exploration of all possible truths from all possible sources

Its fellowship provides strength and encouragement for daily living

Faith, hope, love abide,
these three; but the greatest of these
is love.
1 CORINTHIANS 13:13

There was a long pause then he said quietly to our mutual friend, 'This man's dangerous!' I had hit the nail on the head. He admitted that he had, quite early on in his work, been unable to 'make progress'.

More recently, I was talking to a group of about thirty people in a town in the south-east. For several hours I had talked about psycho-expansion, and we had also done a number of psycho-expansion exercises. There were, among a mixed group in age and profession, several doctors, psychologists and other therapists. I was introduced by a doctor to one of his patients who was also a friend, a girl of about thirty. She remarked that she understood I was also a healer and, upon my admitting that I was, she told me that she had for several years suffered from arthritis which was at the moment particularly painful. Could I do anything?

I said that I would give her some treatment simply by putting my hands on first the head, then the spine and then along to the affected areas. I briefly explained that all one could really prove about healing was that there was a transfer, a flow, of energy through the healer to the patient, which in the case of arthritis was usually felt as heat and tingling. Her right shoulder, her right wrist and her right hip were involved.

As I started I thought of what her symptoms told me about her frustrations. Arthritics tend to be people of fairly fixed opinions about at least *one* thing. They often go just beyond being determined to being stubborn about whatever this idea is. It can, of course, be a general attitude but often just one area of ideas is involved. And then arthritis can set in when there is frustration because they cannot get what they want. Usually it is connected with the behaviour of another or others who just will not see things their way. But the sufferer *knows* that they are right!

Right shoulder? Yes, you are correct. There was some responsibility she wanted but for some reason could not get. The right wrist told me that perhaps there was something almost in her grasp, something she wanted to 'handle' but she had been unable to get her hand on whatever this was. Her right hip told me that she knew where she wanted to go with this 'thing' but she could not even get started. Had the arthritis been in the knee, I would have guessed that she had started making progress but that the progress had come to a halt. Or taken a wrong turning.

I also thought — well, I'm not likely to be able to see her again to give her treatment or to talk to her about causation for many months, if not longer. Should I go into the possible psychosomatic factors involved? I did. I explained briefly the idea of psychosomatics and asked her to think very carefully about what her condition and the parts of the body affected told me. Was there some responsibility which she was very keen to take — something she was very anxious to do — but which she could not 'handle' in the way she would like? In fact, that it was impossible, if not extremely difficult, to get it started?

She did not have to think very hard about it. For two or three years she had been keen to get a Steiner school going in the area. While a number of her friends and associates were in favour of such a venture, she just could not get enough of them to commit themselves — especially financially — so that she had been unable to get it going. I asked her if she had any children and she told me that she had two, one aged three and the other five. 'And, of course,' I said, 'you have been desperately anxious to get the school going so that the eldest could start at the beginning of his school life but — no go.' She agreed. And this was why she was suffering so much just at this time.

I told you earlier that I once had angina. Rather badly too. My heart would seem to become cramped and all the strength would drain from me. Angina sufferers will know exactly what I mean. Walk along on the flat; no problem. Start walking up a slope and the heart begins to seize up. But at one stage with me it did not matter whether I stood still, sat down, laid down; the attacks kept coming. I lost count after forty angina 'attacks' in one morning. After a few weeks withdrawal from normal life the problem eased, but I was taking several types of medication to keep going. I take no medication and I don't have angina now. I'm pretty sure that is because I learned not to 'take things to heart'. In other words, I ceased worrying about what others apparently said or did in opposition to me. I stopped worrying about the opinions of others and, as honestly as I could, acted as I thought correctly in whatever circumstances I found myself. It is absolutely impossible to explain oneself thoroughly to everyone. And even if one could there would still be some who for one reason or another of their own would dislike one. 'My opinion of me' is what matters I decided. It apparently worked.

I have since dealt with many people with heart trouble and

several relatives of patients have actually told me, quite innocently, quite unsuspectingly, that, 'he does take it to heart so' — in connection so very often with a family problem. Perhaps a son or daughter is not behaving as the father thinks they should. Maybe it 'breaks their heart'. Anyway the heart is definitely damaged. They, too, must learn to 'let my people go'.

By the way, perhaps you can help me. Many years ago I read an article concerning a 'post mortem' done on the mummy of the Pharoah who was in conflict with Moses. Apparently the findings

Below: Actions, words, even thoughts, give off ripples which keep spreading and spreading and spreading!
Over: A quiet trip on the river, then half an hour of quiet meditation in the church — if it is open that is.

showed that he had indeed suffered from a disease which actually did cause the tissues of his heart to become less elastic than they should be. The heart was hardened. If you check your Bible, you will see that it refers to Pharoah as having 'hardened his heart' when refusing to let the Jews leave Egypt. I didn't keep the article or I've lost it. I suppose I could do a tracing job and track down those findings but it is a matter of choosing to get on with my work of healing in its various forms.

If *you* remember this article — or if you feel like investigating it — and would let me know I'd be grateful. And we can enter the details in a revised edition of this book! With due credit in your name.

Many years after my own heart trouble had cleared up, I was asked by a hospital consultant, who had called me in on previous occasions, to visit a patient who had had a heart attack and who had an 'erratic' heartbeat which they apparently could not get under control. It had been suggested to the patient, an ex-army colonel, that a healer could perhaps be of some help.

When I went into the ward I saw that he and some of his fellow sufferers around him were linked up to monitors. In his case, on the TV screen could be seen the uneven heartbeat.

After chatting for a few moments, explaining something of what I understood healing to be about, I put my hands over his chest. He could soon feel heat and other sensations. I watched the screen and saw the signals begin to change and even out.

That was six years ago. He is another who comes fairly regularly to our Saturday afternoon sessions; missing a week or two perhaps when he and his wife visit their son in the north.

Some of those who come to the churches on a Saturday or a Sunday have commented that at times it is more like a music hall than a church. That is because I tend to make off the cuff remarks, tell a funny story or two. Often someone in the congregation will correct me or comment; there's 'feedback'. I feel that whereas a church may be the house of God, a house should be a home and a happy home at that. So I encourage not only hearty singing but a spot of hearty laughter, too. 'Hearty'. Twig? Oh yes, we're serious about life and living but there's an adage which I bear in mind: 'life is too important to be taken *too* seriously.' It does help to relax, let go of your problems some of the time and shake the body up a little with laughter.

Chapter 5

The pre-menstrual syndrome, the menopause – and the male menopause.

The mind, via its beliefs, frustrations, thence through the emotional level, can affect the ductless glands, change and block the energy flows and thus cause changes in the body. Physical changes in the body can also have serious effects on the emotions and can influence our beliefs.

I have just come away from giving healing to a patient in an emotional turmoil as a result of the menopause. And it helped to soothe and calm so that I was able to have a chat about what is now called 'pre-menstrual syndrome' and the menopause.

You know, I often get men ringing me and coming to see me in a state of anguished bewilderment because of the irrational behaviour of their wives which they just cannot understand or cope with. Before they have said a couple of dozen words I've spotted the menopausal tension – and any woman who has had severe menopausal problems knows that it is just that; tension. I find, too, that those who have the most difficult time during the menopause have also suffered more than most from pre-menstrual syndrome.

But back to the husband's first contact with me. 'I don't know what to do about my wife. She's constantly ill with something or other. I never know what sort of mood she's going to be in – either furiously angry or in floods of tears and feeling terribly depressed. Sometimes I've only been at work a short while when she phones to say that she feels terribly ill and wants me to come home.' Sometimes, too, say some of the husbands, there are accusations that the husband is having an affair and nothing that is said will convince the wife otherwise. 'She was never like this before. Why should she be so neurotic?'

Sometimes I'm told that the doctor has diagnosed the menopause, given some tablets and said that it will pass. But it doesn't seem to.

If I can, I get them together and we take a trip back in time to

cave-man days. I don't mean that I regress them, I just talk about it.

I'm sure that at some time in your life you've seen a cartoon of a cave-man with a club across his shoulder dragging a girl by the hair. Now why did he do that? I think that this was because the girl played hard to get. Maybe there was no speech even but his intention was clear. She, however, instinctively knew that it wouldn't do her any good to be taken easily. She was fully mobile, perhaps even helped with food gathering or hunting. But if she became pregnant, gave birth and then had to raise a child she couldn't play her part and would have to be looked after – to a degree anyway.

A man can father hundreds of children in the same time that it takes a woman to mother just one. The sexual act was – is – over quickly for a man. But a woman is not truly sexually fulfilled until she has borne, fed and weaned the child.

Probably in those early days primitive man did not consciously connect the sexual act with the birth of children. I think though that instinct was at work. You see, if she gave in easily, he'd be off and away, his job done and feeling satisfied into the bargain. But she wouldn't. Her body's job was just beginning. Instinctively, therefore, she resisted, thus making him want her all the more.

So – the wedding ceremony was a bonk over the nut and with grunts and signs he'd take her to the cave, tell her to get on with the cooking and the housework while he went off to the office – I mean the hunt.

Perhaps, because it was also useful in those days to build up a nice big family tribe to focus loyalty so that other family tribes could be coped with, there was a plurality of wives. And perhaps, too, if a wife didn't produce and assist in the building of the tribe she was thrown out of the group. It happens thus in primitive tribes today. 'Do your job or I don't want you,' grunted the cave husband.

Nowadays we're civilised, rational; there's sexual freedom and equality. Hold it! Hold it? Yes, hang on a bit. What about them there instincts? We still have 'em you know. And that is where I think the problems with pre-menstrual syndrome and the menopause come in. Unfortunately, no matter how free a girl wishes to be, no matter that contraception is relatively easy, there's still that instinctual, emotional biological pattern which causes problems.

'*... a cave-man dragging a girl by the hair.*'

Every month an egg pops down the fallopian tube from the ovary and embeds itself in the wall of the womb. 'Right oh girls,' says womb, 'start all hormonal factories at full output to build up a child!' And the body does just that — only to find after a few days that it is not going to be of much use because that there egg ain't fertile! Right! Chuck it out. And the womb rejects the egg. Period. 'OK body; return to normal. Ease down the factories. Not needed after all.'

'Not needed'? There's a *feeling* of being not needed. There's a *feeling* of failure. The natural progression to pregnancy has been halted. The body is not doing its job. Failure, fear, which soma-psychically (the body affecting the emotions, the mental state) causes the girl to feel that she, the person is a failure. And if she's a failure her husband won't want her. If she's afraid that her husband won't want her, what's the best thing to do to make as sure as possible that he won't want her? Be irritable, irrational, angry. *Then* he won't want her.

And I think something like that does happen. The body is disappointed it has failed to carry out its biological function and that disappointment is carried over to the mental level.

And with the menopause comes the final, complete failure. No longer can she be called a woman in the sense of being a productive female. The sense of failure is stronger and the fear of therefore not being wanted by her mate is stronger.

I'll tell you something; when I've talked with the husband and wife on those lines there is usually a great sense of relief. They understand each other a lot better.

One of the most important points to remember is that when one is afraid one tends to do the very thing to help bring about that of which one is afraid. When you get the time, read the first part of the Book of Job. He said at one point, 'That of which I was afraid has come to pass!' and 'That which I feared has come upon me!' Why? *Because* he feared that his children would go to the dogs, he kept them too much under his thumb. Didn't allow them freedom to learn. He kept too tight a rein on 'em. And what happened? As soon as they could get away from him they had themselves such a good

Maybe there was no speech, but I think the cave-girl played hard to get.

UGH! UGH! THOUSAND TIMES UGH!

time without the ability to see that they were going too far! And that's what we all have to watch out for when we tend to get afraid — that we don't do the very things to bring about that which we fear as did old Job.

No, you don't *necessarily* bring about that which you fear; in fact, I remember listening to an early morning radio broadcast during which the speaker said that he had made a list of all the things he had worried about — and none of them had happened. He made a list of problems that had arisen — and he'd never given a thought to their possible occurrence.

At the moment there are a number of posters on the wall of our clinic. One reads: 'Don't tell me that worrying doesn't do any good. The things I worry about never happen.'

I had just finished writing the above and was talking about the subject to a patient and her husband, who has been a tremendous help in getting our multitudinous activities computerised, when she came back at me with, 'And what about the male menopause then?' Mind you, she said it with a broad smile but I knew she was serious about the subject.

And there *is* something to it you know; with the strong sense of 'failure to achieve' a major ingredient. Just think of all the chaps who, without perhaps having a specific ambition have a forward-looking attitude — forward-*feeling* may be the more correct term. It is a fortunate man — and I must admit that I am one of them — who feels satisfied with life and career when he is fiftyish. Mind you, I'm sixtyish and more satisfied with life than when I was fifty I think!

When you're young you are busy with job, house, family, hobby, all rolling along together. Maybe things don't go any too smoothly at times with one or the other aspect of living, but the average young man keeps going even through divorce perhaps or job loss. But both of those problems hit hard.

I've not been divorced but like practically every married couple we've had some narrow escapes. With both of us being Ariens and fairly strong willed, it sometimes came pretty close. Oh, the times she was going to leave me — and the hours I spent persuading her

I may not always be right, but I am always willing to be forgiven.

not to go. That kind of thing can be a heck of a strain. At one point, many years ago, I decided that if she said again that she was going to leave, well, I'd just have to let her go.

'I'm leaving!' she said, after a strong difference of opinion. 'Right,' I said sorrowfully, 'I'll help you pack.'

She turned, looked at me very straight and said, 'You don't think you're going to get rid of me as easily as all that, do you?'

I had a feeling then that things *might* work out. We've had ups and downs since and have now passed a ruby anniversary.

But, seriously, there are many disappointments in a man's life which react in a similar way to the biological disappointment when a woman does not conceive. I've also been unemployed several times in my younger days, and it was something I found tremendously difficult to cope with, even in my twenties. I was a failure. I wasn't providing for my family. I felt awful. And I know many men must feel the same nowadays. Although in my days of unemployment there wasn't the same degree of social security cushioning there is now and it was indeed a struggle at times.

Now, when a man gets to fifty or so, ambition is not running nearly so strongly in his veins; a number of adverse events of one sort or another have proved that life is more of a struggle than he had bargained for when he was younger and the stars were in his eyes . . . well, depression can set in. A sense of failure can eat into the very bones. And often an escape, an excuse is found in illness of one sort or another. The 'male menopause' has him in its grip. If he has a gripping hobby perhaps he will escape the worst ravages but, unfortunately, a number of hobbies have gone by the board and TVitis has claimed him. And his wife may feel the same perhaps, although she may well have his welfare and looking after the home as her main hobby.

Anyway, if you, sir, or your husband, ma'am, is regularly out of sorts or worse, look into the male menopause syndrome and find a new purpose, a new interest *somewhere, somehow.* There is one.

And you, too, ma'am. Now you've finished your productive bit and the kids don't need you as they used to, *you* find yourself a new purpose along with the old man! See how much better you both feel. It needn't be the same interest, the same purpose. Sometimes it's better if it isn't!

Speaking of 'different interests' reminds me of fallopian tubes! I'll tell you why.

Chapter 6

How relationship problems can cause physical illness. Are you 'of the same kidney' as your wife?

A girl of thirty had made an appointment to see me for healing. She arrived late one morning after driving down from north of Bristol. Her problem was an inflamed left fallopian tube. I gave her healing and we chatted. She was married, happily she said, and had two boys, one seven and the other nearly five. Her husband was a writer. Apparently, in their nine years of married life she and her husband had proved somewhat nomadic. His work took him around a bit and she was quite happy to go with him. It was a little more awkward when the first child arrived but she coped. Her fallopian tube had first caused trouble about a year after their second son was born. She had had medical treatment and it had subsided.

I discovered that between the birth of her second son and a flare up of the fallopian tube trouble they had moved house twice. Each time she had received medical treatment which had been successful – for a while. This was now about the tenth time the problem had recurred.

Do you remember what I said earlier about the left side of the body? Left leg, frustration in connection with progress. Being somewhere where they did not want to be. Left shoulder, frustration in connection with an unwanted responsibility.

I had in the past already dealt with troublesome fallopian tubes and had a good idea what the trouble was, so I asked, 'Does your husband want more children? And you are not so keen?'

I remember she looked a little startled, then answered, 'Oh, we *both* want more children.'

'But?' I said.

And then she began to talk about the family situation and the reservations she had about producing more children because her eldest son had become settled into his school, was getting on well and the second son was about to start his education. And her husband had a couple of months ago told her of plans he had for all of them to do some *real* travelling! A trip around the world. No time limit. He could write anywhere. He could gather masses of material to feed his pen. They could teach the boys as far as formal education went – she had been a teacher. What an opportunity! What a wonderful life they could all have!

She had gone along with the idea but, of course, they couldn't go if this wretched trouble of hers kept cropping up. Nor dare she attempt to have another child. She felt that if she became pregnant complications could set in.

She paused a time or two during the telling. After one pause she said very quietly that in one way she wasn't so keen as he was to travel. Perhaps she was more of a stay-at-home! I found that she was a Virgoan while he was a Sagittarian. Virgo: 'The fruitful one (time of the harvest), home makers, settle down to earth.' Sagittarians like movement – and telling the tale. He'd make a good travelling writer but moving around wasn't quite so natural a thing for her. Their interests were different. Could they be co-ordinated?

I told her something about how the mind and the emotions can affect the body. She was aware that the fallopian tube was where the egg was fertilised before it continued its journey to the womb. If she had had trouble with the right fallopian tube I would have said that she was frustrated because for some reason she could not become pregnant. The trouble with the left fallopian tube told me that although *consciously* she may have wanted more children, *unconsciously* she did not.

In fact, we together discovered that her physical problem helped her in at least two ways. While she was thus handicapped, the settled home life and the children's schooling could continue without interruption. And she didn't have to voice her own doubts about her husband's travelling idea, so there would be no conflict between them.

But, she couldn't continue to escape responsibility by continuing to become 'internally inflamed'. She would have to make decisions – and find the courage to discuss her thoughts and feelings with her husband. Then, I said, I thought that her tube would be unlikely to cause her any further trouble. I told her, too, that while she had felt that the healing treatment had done some good, it was unlikely to be of a permanent nature while she had this unsolved inner conflict.

I saw her again a week later when she said that she had had little trouble but felt that another treatment would be a help. She had discussed her fear with her husband, he had been understanding. Perhaps he could go off by himself for a while? But neither of them was happy about that either.

I saw her again two years later when she brought the eldest son for treatment for a slight chest problem. They were back in England for three months after being abroad for nearly two years. A few travellers' problems but generally they were enjoying themselves hugely.

And their eight-month-old baby girl looked as bonny as any I've seen.

I've dealt with both men and women as far as fertility — or rather lack of it — is concerned. Healing by itself has helped but sometimes discussion is needed to get at deep-seated causes. I

'No act of kindness, however small, is ever wasted.'
Aesop

remember one man who had a low sperm count and did respond to healing. He, as did other men in similar conditions, during healing felt a *cold* flow of energy to the testicles when I placed my hands near the lower abdomen. There were subsequent sperm count tests after healing showing a definite increase; this was especially evident when there was healing treatment two or three hours prior to a test.

On one occasion, a patient told me a dream which we found was very relevant. He dreamt that he was upstairs in a house but heard noises, which he knew emanated from an outhouse attached to his home. He wanted to go and investigate but was stopped from doing so by his mother, who told him that the noise was caused by burglars who would hurt him if he went down there.

After discussion he related the house to himself, his body; 'upstairs' being concern for the higher things of life, while the 'outhouse' represented sex and his sexual organs. Naturally, during puberty in particular, his attention was drawn to that area, but apparently his mother had taught him that sex was dirty and dangerous and to put his mind to 'higher things'. Consequently, he had repressed his sexual feelings, still felt guilty about his desires even after marriage and this, in my opinion, had caused the energy flow to his sexual organs to subtly change so that they did not do their job properly.

Another factor which came out during discussion was that his mother – who was the boss of the household, with father occupying himself with his work and his hobbies – felt that this world was a dreadful place and that life was a struggle. In her opinion, too, it was all going to get worse and it would be a crime to bring more children into the world. All this said while he was a child, of course, and consciously forgotten, but it had psychologically, emotionally and physically affected him. While interpreting the dream he had remembered his mother's attitude and was aware of how he had unrealisingly accepted her 'teaching', her indoctrinations. I think he was alive to the fact that the child which he and his wife produced should not be subjected to such brainwashing.

One of the causes connected with infertility in men is wearing underpants which keep the sexual glands too warm. And girls, too – tights, restricting airflow and not allowing heat to escape, can cause problems such as thrush as some are aware.

A girl who had been married for seven years without producing, and who had had gonadical problems, conceived within two months of having her first healing treatment. In my opinion, I felt that in her case it would not be wise to probe too deeply psychologically. I felt that such an approach could well disturb her and make her worse. Some just don't feel mentally strong enough to cope with too much knowledge of themselves over too short a period. She had healing twice a week for two months. Quiet, soothing healing which helped her to become more and more relaxed and, without her being too aware of what had happened, she let go of deep-seated fears which had caused her infertility.

I remember, too, spending a day at Tiverton Natural Health Centre, where I gave several talks and demonstrations on healing. During the afternoon and the evening sessions two young ladies were among those present but, even though I invited them to sample the treatment, they declined saying that they were just interested observers. Until, just after eleven p.m. when most had gone and I was just preparing to leave for an hour and a half's drive home, then they plucked up courage to tell me that they both wanted to have babies but they had fallopian tube trouble — the right rube.

I told them that I couldn't do any more that night but invited them to Moretonhampstead to my usual Sunday afternoon session. They duly came, several times, had treatment and within a year brought their new babies to church.

In their case we didn't have very much personal discussion but they did come to psycho-expansion, learnt something about themselves and released a lot of tension and anxiety. One major fact was, I think, that they were both trying too hard. And were afraid of failure. So — they failed until they forgot their fears.

I have dealt with a number of individual victims of rape and incest with their resultant psychological and physical problems, but when I was for the first time requested by a medical practitioner to talk to the then newly-formed 'Rape Crisis' group, I was somewhat at a loss to think of what to say. When the day of the talk came I still hadn't the vaguest idea of how to approach the victims of rape all gathered together at a meeting, so I decided to get to the rendezvous half an hour early and see if I could get a lead.

They were mostly quite young with two or three over forty perhaps. I was introduced — I went as a psychotherapist, not a minister, by the way — and I launched into a talk on psychosomatics. We were all sitting, me included, and the situation was somewhat

Take life
one day
at a time.

informal. After about ten minutes, one of the girls broke in rather sharply with, 'What's all this got to do with us?'

'Hang on a bit and you'll find out,' I answered and I continued to talk about the links between various emotions, fears and how they affected us physically. I hadn't mentioned the sexual organs, fallopian tubes, etc. until I came out with, 'Now, I would say that in the case of rape two physical problems could arise, perhaps shortly after the event or perhaps some months afterwards. Trouble with, say inflammation of, the left fallopian tube and kidney trouble of some sort, left or right or both.'

Every woman there had had one or the other after being raped and in some cases had suffered with left fallopian tube trouble and kidney trouble as well. The girl who had broken in had herself suffered from both.

'But why? How can that be?' They were, to say the least, somewhat surprised to find that they had *all* without exception, physically suffered in the same way. Yes, in some cases there was cystitis, thrush too, and other genito-urinary problems.

Why kidneys? I'll tell you. For several years after I'd cottoned on to this psycho-physical link-up, I couldn't figure out the significance of the kidney though I was aware of the fact that where a relationship problem was very much in a person's mind, then they also had a kidney problem.

Then one day I remembered a saying which was fairly common in the days of my childhood, but which is seldom heard these days. It was said of two people who were alike in some way; usually it was said of those who were often in trouble and were in each other's company a lot. 'Ah,' someone would say, 'those two are of the same kidney', meaning there was a relationship, or 'those two aren't of the same kidney' would be said of perhaps a man and his wife who were not well matched.

And when I looked up 'kidney' in Brewer's *The Dictionary of Phrase and Fable*, I found 'Kidney. Men of another kidney or of the same kidney. The reins or kidneys were even by the Jews supposed to be the seat of the affections.' If you are a parapsychologist and immediately think of the link with the chemical ether, may I say that I am aware of this but it is beyond the scope of this book.

Barney by Jad.

I explained to the girls of the Rape Crisis group how, in the past, I had dealt with individual cases where for some reason there had been the desire *not* to have a child: and the left fallopian tube had been affected in some way. Who wants to have a rapist's child?

But there was more to it than that. I was aware from past experience that girls who have been forced into sexual intercourse against their will will still feel ashamed afterwards. And it is even worse when a total stranger is involved – in many rape cases the victim knows the attacker. Even if they did not in any way, shape or form invite an attack, they still feel guilt. And they are afraid, too, that their marital partner is ashamed. No matter how much he protests that all is well between them, there is a damaged relationship. At least, that is the *fear* of the girl so very often, hence the kidney trouble.

But as I explained, what one fears, what one believes is not necessarily true. If you believe something to be true, you'll be able to see the evidence of its truth in many ways, while being totally unable to see evidence opposing your fear or belief. The power of hypnosis is not simply suggestion, the power is *belief* in the validity of the suggestion. And you, no doubt, are aware of the power of hypnosis.

What is needed, I pointed out, is a suspension of belief. Really honestly for some little while – no matter *what* evidence you can see, try and then try again to see evidence opposing your belief that your relationship is on the rocks. You'll begin to relax and get it all together again. And the kidney problem should correct itself.

Again, treat the physical problem – medically, with healing, or both – and the kidney trouble clears up, so the relationship problem should improve *if* the kidney sufferer is provoking the relationship problem because of fear.

If there is a relationship problem – if the 'two are not of the same kidney' – then, when the position is accepted – not just 'put up with' but *accepted with equanimity* and the negative emotional factor is dealt with – then, again, the kidney problem should clear up. I have known cases, too, where there has been kidney trouble which has completely cleared up after a divorce.

I watched a continuing newspaper story over a period of weeks when a teenaged girl eloped with a fellow who was not of the best of characters. The father appealed through the media for her to come home but there was no response. Some weeks later it was reported that the father was suffering from kidney failure. The daughter apparently saw the newspaper report, returned home and decided to leave her lover. The father's kidneys returned to working order.

There has been a great deal of controversy over the use of fertility drugs, which often result in multiple births, in vitro fertilisation — 'test tube' babies — and also surrogate motherhood and artificial insemination by donor. Some who have contemplated such moves have come to us for treatment. I am aware of only one couple — out of about a dozen total — who did not have a child after consultation and the simplest of treatment such as described.

Chapter 7

Is your problem facing up to speaking your mind?

'Facing up to the truth' when we want to avoid doing so – possibly through fear of the consequences – is not easy, which reminds me of a number of 'facial problems'.

I was asked by a company director to see one of his key workers, who frequently suffered from severe and disabling facial eczema. When I saw him it was really dreadful, bleeding and oozing and dripping from his face. There was no way he could continue his work while in such a condition. His employer had, over the years, paid for him to be treated by a number of experts of one sort or another. He had travelled to London and other parts of the country for advice and treatment and, while it would clear up for a time, it would before long re-occur and put him completely out of action.

The eczema was all around his mouth and chin, causing him great difficulty in both eating and also in speaking. While healing treatment helped to soothe, I was of the opinion that the parts of the face affected indicated that probably he was 'erupting' because somehow he could not gather up enough courage to 'stick his chin out'. Was he afraid of saying something to some particular person? It is interesting to note that 'ECZEMA' is of Greek origin, *EK* out, *ZEEN* to boil.

We talked – as best we could. His wife had not come with him and I understood that he was quite sure that she would *never* come with him to see me. For what reason he could not or would not say. But some weeks later I had occasion to travel in his direction and I called in and met them both together.

I began to get the picture. Boy! Could she talk! Non-stop and

The healing beauty and the healing quality of the ocean.

nobody and nothing was right about anything. He couldn't get a word in edgeways. She was particularly vitriolic about his boss and, obviously, she did not like her husband having to work for him. I've met some tough cookies in my time, but this one — well!

I summed up the situation. Of course! He didn't have the ability to oppose the tirades from his wife. He just wasn't strong enough in a number of ways. And I thought, too, how in a strange way this eczema was useful to him! He couldn't speak up, so he couldn't get into trouble by answering back. He couldn't get into trouble by working for someone of whom his wife so strongly disapproved. I don't think she would approve of anyone for whom he worked. I don't think she approved of anything at all.

And I felt that she wasn't going to approve of me, especially if I did what I had in mind to do. Still, I thought, as *her* thoughts were still being voiced in full throttle while she busied herself with various things in the kitchen, if she beats me with a frying pan it won't be the first time I've been bopped by an irascible female!

I managed to stop the flow and get her to sit and keep quiet. It wasn't easy. She was angry; it was none of my business, I could get out of her house . . . it was all thrown at me verbally – but no saucepans – before I did persuade her to stop and listen. As soon as she did stop, she burst into tears, which appeared to absolutely astound her husband. He told me on another occasion that he had definitely never ever seen her cry before. Instructive in itself.

While I had the opportunity, I told them both exactly what I thought his and their problem was. Basically, of course, fear. And through the manifestation of fear they were really ripping apart their lives. I did, after nearly two hours, leave them knowing that they had *begun* to discuss the situation. I didn't inform the company director, who, on several later occasions, pressed me hard to tell him how his employee had finally managed to rid himself of his dreadful eczema. But there obviously wasn't any 'boiling over' any more.

A local government officer drove over fifty miles to see me about his eczema. Again, around the mouth, but also his right hand was badly affected. He normally had to deal with the public but it was not possible to do so in such a state. I gave healing treatment and also some herbal ointment which I had made up. The treatments soothed but I felt disinclined to say *too* much about the psychogenic factors until after the third treatment. Then I began to talk about the influence of the emotions and I gave him a copy of a talk I'd given to some pharmacists on psychosomatic medicine. The next time he came there was a slight improvement, and he asked me a few questions about psychosomatics. He could not easily relate his condition to an emotional factor or frustration.

'Is there anyone that you would like to say something to but feel that you just – for what reason I don't know – dare not do so? It may well be connected with a situation which you know only too well how it should be handled but you are, for some reason, frustrated and stopped from handling it in the way you *are* certain is right?'

'Strallops!' he muttered. At least that's what I thought he said, but wasn't *quite* sure.

'Pardon?', I said.

'Never mind,' he said, 'I know what you're talking about!' And he left it at that.

'Or,' I said, 'it may possibly be a person whom you feel you cannot "handle" in the way you wish. But,' I continued hurriedly, 'I don't have to know the details. It's enough that you have clues yourself as to how your frustration is causing you to erupt in this particular way.'

He remained quiet, but politely said, 'Goodnight and thank you' when leaving. I wondered if I would, in fact, see him again. As it was, other therapists in our clinic gave him treatment before I personally saw him again about two weeks later. The eczema had entirely disappeared from the face and the hand was almost cleared up. Interestingly enough, the little finger of his right hand was, however, worse! He was having treatment in the main healing room when I looked in and expressed pleasure at his improvement. I asked if he could spare me a few minutes in the 'insulting room' when he was free.

When he came in I said, 'It was a person then — that you had difficulty in handling?' His eyebrows raised quizzically but he said nothing. 'I say that,' I said, 'because whatever tactics you were using before, which were frustrated, you may have changed — but you're still not getting the results you want.'

'I don't follow,' he said.

'Well, your right little finger is worse than it was. Who are you trying to twist round your little finger? And failing to succeed. No, I don't want you to tell me. I'm simply pointing out that you seem to be up against someone who is as determined as you are to have their own way. You must be spending a great deal of time on attempting to win. Are you sure it's not just false pride keeping you at it?'

'Humph,' he grunted.

'No,' I said, 'personally, *I* don't want to know. But one can waste an awful lot of one's life attempting to make another or others behave as you would like them to. But — and please think carefully — is it in the first place your *business* to try and make them behave as you

Jack Pickup's oil painting of Jesus calming the storm with, below, Rod Mason and his Jass Band calming the Sunday morning congregation at Plymouth Unitarian Church with sweet music.

wish them to? And in the second place, is it worth all the probably wasted time and effort and, as in your case, physical discomfort?' He smiled, thanked me coolly but politely, and went on his way.

I saw him some months later, quite by chance, in the town in which he worked, during the lunch hour. We greeted each other, shook hands, said what gorgeous weather we'd been having. I noted that he looked more relaxed, had a better complexion and was about to wend my way without making any comment about his health, when he gave me a slow grin and lifted up his left hand to show me a little — just a little — eczema on his left little finger. I grinned back at him and he said, 'I know. She is trying to twist me around *her* little finger. And I know it, I'm not having it — but I'm not reacting *too* much.'

Thinking about what he had said, while partaking of my ploughman's lunch, I had to grin.

Chapter 8

According to your belief . . .

I've told you a few, just a few, of the hundreds of cases I'd like to tell you about - there are some I couldn't and wouldn't like to tell you about - which I'm sure would fascinate and enlighten you. You've read how healing, 'laying on of hands' or 'Diatronic therapy' (Healing through Energy) can, without a word being spoken, assist the patient to counteract the physical problem from which he or she suffers. You've read, too, how, in my opinion, with which many others do not agree, the beliefs and attitudes of mind, habits of thought with consequent emotions affect the flows of energy in the body. Energies via the healer can change this flow, which in turn can soma-psychically affect the emotions and thinking patterns of the patient. 'Soothing' or 'comforting' are two of the most common expressions used during a 'healing' session.

You've read, too, of how some can, to some degree or other, relate their physical problems to their emotional problems and through counselling can be helped to change their thought patterns to a more helpful one, both for themselves and others.

To assist a growing understanding of themselves, why they have this or that physical or emotional problem, we also have group therapy of different types. All of these, while perhaps having a lighthearted and even a 'fun' content or approach, are also designed to help those partaking learn step by step something about themselves which will help them to eventually shed the physical and emotional problem.

In the case of 'Cancer Compassion', which is for cancer sufferers and also at least one family member as a support, we have to tread delicately perhaps because of the high death fear element. But gradually, with learning to relax, to help visualise away the cancer, plus gentle but uplifting music and dietary and other aids, smiles do grow. I shall go into detail a little later on about visualisation.

PSYCHO EXPANSION ©

Of course, there are other serious problems which weigh heavily on some, who find it almost impossible at first to become light-hearted. In the stress release groups, where again some attend with another member of the family as support, music, guided visual meditation all play their part in relaxing the participants and helping them to return to a fuller and more enjoyable life.

We have, too, special one day groups, which we refer to as 'A Day of Discovery!' in which all sorts of 'exercises', gentle mental exercises, help those taking part to lift up their hearts and learn *something* about how to help themselves.

I suppose that the groups which have caught the attention of radio, television and the Press are the psycho-expansion groups, primarily because a number of the exercises include 'regression' and those taking part apparently experience 'living' an episode in what could be a past life. These episodes are very real to the experiencer but there is no way one can describe fully to another just what is experienced.

In the last television programme made by TSW and later networked, Judy Spiers, the interviewer said, 'But it will be said by a great many people that this is simply illusion.' I could only answer 'Yes.' I said no more. It was true; many people do say that. Those who experience psycho-expansion regression exercises do sometimes think that they have an active imagination - at first; while some, right from the start, are quite convinced that they are indeed re-living an episode from a previous incarnation.

We not only 'travel in time' - in psycho-expansion; there are many exercises we do which are designed to 'expand the ability of the psyche' which is why we use the term 'pyscho-expansion'.

I'm afraid that some years ago we had to copyright the term and logo *(above left)*: because we found that one or two people who had been to a few sessions picked up something of the technique, then began running groups saying in some cases that they had trained with us.

One has to be extremely careful, as I've learned in over thirty years work helping others to know themselves even just a little more. The mind is a tender flower which has to be treated gently and kindly. I'm afraid that I've not been very happy with some of the hard hitting 'encounter group' type of work, when the emotions are stirred up and banged around. I've had some exeperience of it and it doesn't worry me personally in the least, but I've seen the adverse effect upon *some*.

In my opinion we can get quite enough emotional turmoil in day-to-day living without *artificially* creating negative emotional states. Mind you, some can and do benefit from such groups. I have myself. And those who wish to have 'encounters' or partake in such groups as Exegesis are welcome to do so. But I prefer the gentler approach with patients and students.

It is true that some who join in pyscho-expansion groups do uncover some things about themselves in this life and apparent past lives which are painful. If they wish to tell others in the group or the group leader or me, they can do so; and we'll try to help them understand and cope. But no other person need know anything at all about what they have experienced and written in their notes. And we deliberately keep the atmosphere light and happy and the great majority of the participants find the sessions fun. They actually enjoy them! 'Better than television' is a remark that has been made by many.

We do not use hypnosis. No one, as in ordinary hypnotic sessions, is *told* what to experience. Neither are any of the exercises done with the 'force' such as that used by Joe Keaton, whom you have probably seen on television. It is a gentle technique and *no one has to do anything that they do not want to.* Admittedly, some do fall asleep occasionally during the exercises but it is simply because they are relaxed, *not* because they have been hypnotised.

What is actually occurring during the gradual progression of the exercises is *de*-hypnotisation. The process does in fact help individuals to learn to become aware of the 'conditioning' of their minds which has taken place during this life – and possibly during previous lives. In a later chapter I will, however, tell you of an even *easier* way to expand the ability of the mind.

I think I should warn you at this point that the rest of this chapter is not just an easy, quick read! It needs careful consideration. If you *do* find it tough going, skip it, go on to the next chapter and come back to this one later.

What I want to do is look at hypnotism a little more closely and explain why I am not happy about using hypnosis.

It is so often said that it is not fully understood how hypnotism works. It is also repeatedly said that the power of hypnotism lies in 'suggestion'. If we look at what occurs we will, in fact, discover that the power lies not in suggestion but in the *acceptance* of the suggestion, the *belief* in its validity.

In a theatre say, the hypnotist can tell perhaps five hundred people to place their hands on their heads and interlock their fingers. He can tell them to push their fingers tighter and tighter together and then say, 'Now you cannot pull them apart!' After a slight pause he will say, 'Now take your hands down.' Perhaps 490 will be able to do so with ten unable, because they have, while still conscious, believed the hypnotist. These ten he will then call upon to go on stage.He will then *tell* them that they now find it quite easy to lower their hands and put them by their sides. Again, they will believe him and do so. He may quickly give more simple suggestions which they *believe* easily and which strengthens their capability of believing other suggestions, which are not quite so ordinary.

He can then give them, for example, an onion but *tell* them it is an apple, which they will enjoy eating. After which he can tell them to take a bite. They again *believe* him, take a bite from the onion, but because of their belief they will find that their *sensations* are those not which would result from biting into an onion but those which would normally result from taking a bite from an apple. Sensations and perceptions are then the results, not of actuality but of belief.

He can tell them, too, that after they return to their seats when a certain word is spoken or when a certain tune is played by the orchestra or the pianist that their seats will become red hot. When the word is spoken or the tune is played, they do indeed leap to their feet because their seats do feel red hot. Again, it is *belief* which has caused the sensation.

In hypnotic therapy a different, more leisurely technique can be used. The hypnotist can suggest that the room is getting warmer and warmer and that the subject is becoming more and more sleepy. If those suggestions are accepted, believed to some degree to be true, then indeed the subject becomes more and more sleepy, reaching the 'hypnagogic' level when his own reasoning, his judgment is keyed out, just as it is when we drift off to sleep. When lying down in bed we may be aware of thoughts which gradually become quiescent until we are no longer actually 'thinking', but images become visible and we then drift further into dream sleep.

In hypnotism, when the subject has been relaxed to this state, suggestions are then made which, because the subject's own judgment is suspended, are accepted and then acted upon as if the subject had formed the conclusion, the belief, for himself, *except* where it clashes with an already formed belief or conclusion. Then there would be a tendency to come back to full consciousness in order to bring in the judgment to decide between the two ideas.

There is usually, in fact, an emotional reaction because with two opposing ideas of perhaps fairly equal strength there may be difficulty in coming to a decision and the subject is, for a while at least, in a neurotic condition of indecision. Usually when this kind of thing occurs under hypnosis, there is a tendency for confusion and an inability to remember the new suggestion presented.

When, after weighing pros and cons for a short or long time, making a decision that 'this is correct', we come to a conclusion - we conclude thinking; we have finished with our judgment and have formed a belief. We are then effectively self-hypnotised. Just as the hypnotic subject has believed that the onion is an apple and his senses are distorted, actuality is distorted, *so it is with each one of us when we form a conclusive belief.* We, because of our conditioned, hypnotised state, cannot see evidence which conflicts with our belief. The factual evidence opposing our beliefs just does not register in our minds.

Before reaching an age when we are able to reason, we simply and easily accept what 'is' in our environment. And we also as young children accept easily what we are told by parents and then by

I would admit
my faults
if I
had
any.

others around us, which is when the confusion starts, of course, because an awful lot of conflicting behaviour and statements are registered. Confusion is there if parents tell a child how he or she should behave and then the parents row and exhibit unhappiness. How can a child follow the teachings of adults who are obviously unhappy? So they tend not to follow their parents' advice. There is a much greater tendency to follow the advice of parents when there is a happy and peaceful atmosphere in the home. Obvious? Well - I don't know. Think over your own experience.

Our own emotions - the motions, the movements of our feelings - give us clues and there are many types of emotions which, however, can be placed in two main categories: 'pleasant' and 'unpleasant'.

A pleasant emotion is based upon a desire to continue with - or repeat - something which I have concluded (believed) is right. For *me.* This I believe is how my world should be. In fact, what I am really doing, albeit in a small way, is to feel relief and satisfaction in the discovery - the 'apparent' discovery because my belief may not be true - that my judgment is correct. I am relieved to find that I *can* think correctly. That I am sane.

An unpleasant emotion is based upon a desire to escape from or avoid a repetition of something which I judge to be wrong for 'me'. And that which is wrong is so very often connected with the behaviour of another or others. Here, until, if, I can change the circumstances, I am up against the fear, the belief that maybe my judgment is wrong. That maybe I cannot think properly, reasonably, sanely.

In both pleasant and unpleasant emotions, however, we do not think into the situation with enough objectivity to see the matter clearly. In the case of a pleasant emotion; OK! Carry on! All's well — but is it. In the case of an unpleasant emotion, while we *may* be able to change the circumstances to our liking, we have still gone along with the belief that that which occurred to bring about an unpleasant emotion was not according to our judgment of what should be. If we cannot change the circumstances, we may become used to the new circumstances without having moved our belief structure one iota. So we have not really opened our mind. We have not really learnt anything. We certainly have not moved from the egotistic belief that our judgment was correct. We still, in fact, continue to do what Adam and Eve are reported to have done; we 'eat of the fruit of the tree of knowledge of good and evil'. This in spite of the teaching of great masters that *we* should not rely upon our own judgment of

'One can never "conclude" thinking, searching . . .'

what or whom is right or wrong. We still prefer to suffer mentally, emotionally and physically, as I have pointed out in previous chapters, because *we* do not wish to change our belief pattern - our character.

It is my understanding 'at this present moment in time' through the experiences and lessons of my life that if one seeks one does indeed find. But - and it's a very big BUT! - if you at any point say, 'I have found all I want to find,' and then discontinue seeking, then you *cease* to find. The mind, life, spiritual growth *I understand* — you may have proof of the opposite, which I would be extremely interested in hearing — is never static, always in a state of flux. One can never 'conclude' thinking, searching, keeping a mind open for new evidence every moment.

If *you* do not wish to change that's OK!

You *would* like to change? You've tried but found it too difficult? Let me describe to you a way which you just *might* find successful.

Chapter 9

Do you know what you want?

'Pam,' he said.

'Pardon?' I said.

'Pam – P A M,' he said.

We both knew several Pams but my mind flew to Pam Canter, the musical Pam, because the speaker was Barry Westcott, one of my favourite people. He had called in for the third time that week while he was in Plymouth as musical director of *The Wind in the Willows*, showing at the Theatre Royal. I had not seen him personally for five years – although I had seen him on television conducting an orchestra at a rehearsal for a West End show.

'Pam who?' I asked.

'Not a girl,' he said. 'Pam – P A M – Positive Attitude of Mind. That's what is important.'

'Ah!' I said, having rumbled what he was on about. We'd been talking about his work and my work and he had re-read something I'd written just before I met him for the first time. And I knew, too, that he had discovered 'PAM' for himself and quietly applied it over the years.

In 1954 I was asked to put down on paper some of the things I had been saying at talks I had been giving in the Westcountry. One leaflet I wrote then has been reprinted many times since. It was entitled, 'Do You Know What You Want?' It had been suggested by some that the title should be, 'How To Get What You Want!' But I favoured the former. I'll leave you to decide between the two titles because I'm going to quote from it at length.

'If you are young you may have a vague idea of "getting on" in life. If you are not so young you may not wish to "get on" but you may feel that if you "only had this or that" you would be more contented and your life would be happier.

'Do you know what it is that you want? Or where your ambition lies? Have you got the picture of it clear in your mind? If you have all is well. If you do want to get somewhere and don't know quite where, you had better make up your mind quickly. If you are content with what you have, you are lucky because you are one in a million.

'When I asked you if you had the "picture clear in your mind", did you consider it just another phrase without real meaning?

'Right, let us get down to the mechanics of that phrase.

'Here is an experiment which all of you can carry out – but unless you can concentrate very well with the radio playing or other people talking, I should not attempt it under those conditions. Try and get in as peaceful a spot as possible and when you are swinging your eyes – as explained in the following instructions – do not let other thoughts creep in. Simply concentrate on the backwards and forwards or the up and down motions.

'Look at this drawing of a circle containing a cross.

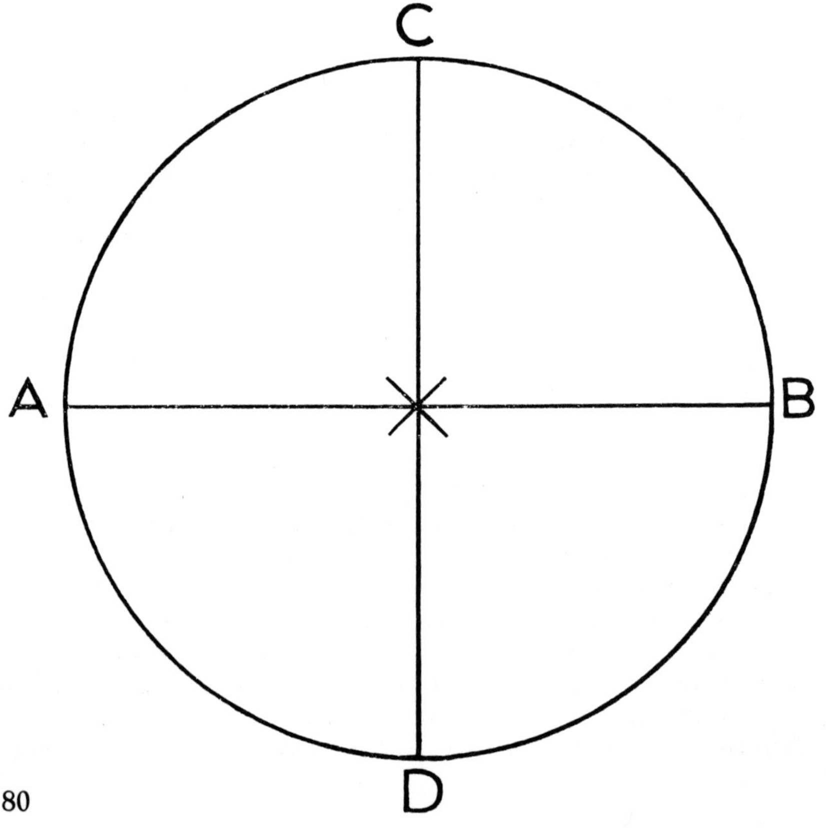

'Get a pencil, a piece of cotton about a foot long and a fairly heavy button. Make a fishing rod of it with the button as the fish. Place the paper on the table in front of you and hold the rod so that the button is in a line between the centre of the cross and your eyes. Keep your elbow away from your side and keep your hand as still as you possibly can. Now – think of the button swinging between A and B and at the same time let your eyes swing backwards and forwards between A and B. You will find that after a while the button begins to swing along the same line.

'Now alter your thought and the direction of your eyes to between C and D. You will find that although you are still making no voluntary movement with your hand the button gradually alters its swing to between C and D. This second movement may take a little longer because your attention will naturally be attracted by the pendulum swinging the other way. Nevertheless keep your thoughts fixed on the swing between C and D and let your eyes swing up and down and the pendulum will do as you think! Switch your thoughts once more and let your thoughts and your eyes run in a circle right round the perimeter. You will find that the pendulum follows. Now watch the centre of the cross quite steadily and think of the pendulum remaining quite still and very soon it will come to rest.

'After a few tries the pendulum will react to you using thought alone. It will not be necessary for you to look at the line or swing your eyes. You will be able to do it – quite literally – with your eyes shut!

'What has this to do with getting what you want? Simply this: you had your thoughts concentrated on the swinging motion and as a result of concentration on this one idea it came true. When you altered your thoughts and concentrated on a new idea that eventually came true also.

'Here is the explanation. You have a conscious mind which is your reasoning, thinking mind. You also have a sub-conscious mind which is the storehouse of all that you have learnt and which is your controller. It controls every atom of your physical body and reacts on your conscious mind.

'In your normal everyday waking life your sub-conscious mind controls you only upon the instructions of your conscious mind. This statement seems quite straightforward and the process appears to be perfectly simple. In fact it is far more simple than most of us realise – which is just where we have been making a great mistake. Take for example the pendulum. You thought a thought again and again, passing the instruction to your sub-conscious mind. In effect your sub-conscious said: "Those are your orders, I'll carry them out." And it sent the message down the nerves of your arm and your hand to make the pendulum swing whichever way you thought.

'You see? You didn't have to make any undue physical effort to do it. In fact you probably didn't realise that you were making a physical effort at all. You simply thought about it and with the minimum of movement – extremely delicately controlled by the sub-conscious mind – it came true. If you consciously make a physical effort to swing the pendulum the control – especially the change from one direction to another – is to say the least – somewhat clumsier.

'Dependent upon the goal, to control your sub-conscious you must have a relatively strong thought or idea which in the case of the pendulum was built up by continually repeating the same thought for but a few moments without letting other thoughts intervene.

'The stronger the thought, or in other words the clearer the picture in your mind, of what you want done the quicker your sub-conscious brings it about.

'I can just imagine someone saying: "Perhaps it will work with a parlour trick like that but how on earth could it possibly affect me and my ambitions?" I'll tell you. You train your sub-conscious with your thoughts. The way in which you think determines the type of person you will be – and where you will get in life. What you have to do is to control your thoughts, cutting out all those which are unnecessary or even detrimental to your living the kind of life you prefer.

'If there was a girder thirty feet long and eighteen inches wide placed on the ground you would be able to walk from one end to the other comfortably. If this girder was placed between the roofs of two skyscrapers you would probably not be able even to start walking along the girder. Why not? Simply because you have the strong thought in your mind of yourself falling. If you were to attempt to cross, your sub-conscious would, upon the instruction of this strong thought – amplified by fear – cause you to lose your balance and fall to your death.

'How is it that steeplejacks and acrobats can perform feats similar to this with ease? They have trained their minds with thoughts of getting across quite safely. They have cut out of their minds any thoughts detrimental to their safety and they expect to succeed. That is the idea – the belief – which they hold.

'By exactly the same process the stronger the thought of success in your conscious mind the easier it is to attain success. Your sub-conscious will make sure that you do the right things.

'The stronger the thought of failure the quicker will you fail for again your sub-conscious will cause you to do the right things – to achieve failure!

'Arnold Bennett – the author of *The Card* – has something to say about "Success" in his book *Mental Efficiency*. On page 119 he says: "Are successful men more industrious, frugal and intelligent than men who are not successful? I maintain that they are not, and I have studied successful men at close quarters. One of the commonest characteristics of the successful man is his idleness, his immense capacity for wasting time. I stoutly assert that as a rule successful men are by habit comparatively idle. As for frugality, it is practically unknown among the successful classes; this statement applies with particular force to financiers. As for intelligence, I have over and over again been startled by the lack of intelligence in successful men. They are indeed capable of stupidities that would be the ruin of a plain clerk. And much of the talk in those circles which surround the successful man is devoted to the enumeration of instances of his lack of intelligence . . . They are the least methodical of creatures."

'On page 125 he says: "How comes it that men without any other talent possess a mysterious and indefinable talent to succeed? Well, it seems to me that such men always display certain characteristics, and the chief of these characteristics is the continual, insatiable wish to succeed. We others are not so preoccupied. We dream of success at intervals, but we have not the passion for success . . ."

'You see? They can have all the disadvantages – they can be morons but with the constant picture in their minds of success they get to the top! Whether or not they are happy people is another question which we'll deal with later.

'Arnold Bennett was referring to one type of successful man. One without any talent whatsoever. He mentions others who get there by sheer merit, as he calls it and by "chance". Would any of them have got to the top if they had not had the belief in themselves – if they had not had the picture in their minds of themselves as successes?

'Here are two real life examples; the first of a failure the second of a success.

'A daily newspaper reported that a London secretary had been almost constantly thinking and worrying about losing her job through ill health. Although she was in good health she allowed this thought to recur until it had built up into a belief with the result that definite instructions were passed to her sub-conscious mind, instructions to the effect that she must lose her job through ill health. Her sub-conscious – always obedient – caused her to commit suicide. When dead one can scarcely be described as healthy and obviously it is impossible to carry on working.'

I then mention Sir Charles Forte, who now owns far more than he did in 1954! He started in business by buying a gown shop in Regent Street. He put a bar in it, sold milk drinks, and called it, 'The Meadow Milk Bar'.

In 'Do You Know What You Want?' I said: 'How did he THINK to get where he is now? According to a Sunday newspaper he said this, "You must believe in what you do to succeed and trust the people around you just as they should trust you. Determination is another point . . ."

'Notice the words "believe" and "determination". The first you've seen in action with the pendulum – you built up a belief and it came true. My dictionary defines "determination" as "fixedness of purpose". In other words concentration – which is what you used to fix your belief when operating the pendulum.

'As for his statement that you should trust the people around you just as they should trust you, well, you'll learn plenty of truisms like that if you act upon the promptings of your sub-conscious mind, your intuition. If, when you first meet a man, you don't trust him, because you are afraid of his beating you, he will feel it, either by his intuition or by some definite indication which you will give. He will act accordingly. His sub-conscious will, in effect, say: "Hmmm. This chap doesn't trust me. I know that I am a fair man so if he doesn't trust me then he must be judging by his own standards, which are obviously low. Right. No deal!"

'In a nutshell – if you want to receive you must first of all give in thought and deed. If you want co-operation you must first be willing to co-operate completely unselfishly – without thought of gain. You do this by thinking charitably in the first place, so that your sub-conscious will cause you to act charitably.

'To summarise: First of all you will find that it is completely useless to attempt to succeed at anything at all if you consciously allow thoughts of failure or the sense of depression to remain in your mind. Think of something positive and cheerful – BE OPTIMISTIC! – and you will cancel the wrong thoughts out.

'Secondly: don't try too hard for success; just confidently hope and expect it to arrive. If you try and force things you are liable to make mistakes and be clumsy over it – just as you were when you consciously tried to swing the pendulum. The same law is in force, you see; if you believe that the job in hand is hard, then your sub-conscious will see that you do the wrong things, in order to make it hard! You can safely leave it to your sub-conscious mind to prompt you and give you ideas. You will know when to make a move and when to sit tight and do nothing.

'Thirdly: keep on thinking of yourself as you wish to be – completely ignoring the failures you have had in the past.

'Fourthly: make sure of your goal before you allow your sub-conscious to guide you on your way. Ask yourself quite honestly what it is you want – and why you want it! Do you want to be wealthy? Why? Because being wealthy you think that you will then be happy? Do you want to be famous – as a musician or an athlete? Why? – Because it'll make you happy? That's the real goal – HAPPINESS! That's what you are really after!

'So: see yourself as a really happy and contented person. Keep that thought in your mind and that is just what you will become. If it is necessary for you to have wealth or to be a successful politician to attain that state of mind, then you will get what is necessary – your sub-conscious will see to that.

'And remember the rules to get there. The constant thought builds up into FAITH. The Hope and Expectancy keep the faith going, and – most important of all – the CHARITABLE thought and outlook to others guides it in the right direction!

'Think of Faith as a mighty engine – which it is. Consider Hope the fuel. Right, now you can move; now you can get somewhere. But where? That depends upon the steering gear – Unselfishness or Love.

'Did I hear you say "FAITH, HOPE and LOVE again?" Quite right. Do you see how it works?

'ONE VERY IMPORTANT POINT, WHEN ONE CHANGES ONE'S THINKING FROM WHATEVER IT IS TO WHOLLY POSITIVE THINKING THEN THERE IS A LIKELIHOOD OF INITIAL UPSETS. Things may appear to get worse for a while. All the previous fears, doubts, worries and errors in thinking – all the previous wrong instructions to the sub-conscious mind – seem to set up a reaction. It is as if they rise to the surface from the sub-conscious like scum to be skimmed off.

'You can liken this to starting a new job. You were quite familiar with the routine of the old one when you made up your mind to leave it and start a new one. When you start the new one some things are bound to be difficult because you have to build up an entirely different routine. You have to form new habits of thought in connection with the new job. But you don't give up, you keep at it until the job is plain sailing.

'Some people have given up at this stage because they have felt that they should get perfect results straight away. They thought that the new job would be absolutely automatic but instead of things being easier they apparently became worse! The key word is – "apparently". They are not becoming worse in reality. This is a sort of purifying process and if you accept it as such and KNOW that things will straighten out and become smoother they are bound to do so. Keep your faith – then you will be well on your way to the target.

'Now – I suggest that if you have read this straight through without trying the experiment with the pendulum, you try the experiment and make sure that it really does work. If you have had no conscious experience of your own of the power of thought then try the pendulum and see for yourself just how it does work.

'Also jot down on a piece of paper your own thoughts concerning all that you have read. Did you think negatively or positively before reading this pamphlet? Or were you neither one or the other but a "Passive" type allowing yourself to drift first one way and then another?

'Can you remember any specific "co-incidences" in your own life when a result followed a trend of thought – either good or bad?

'Think on these things and remember to be positive in future. Relax – and act as if you were already a happy, contented person! Build up a real idea or belief of yourself in that state and as you carry on with your ordinary affairs watch how things sort themselves out.

'Remember! – that reading about an idea and accepting it as true is useless unless action is taken! IF YOU BELIEVE THAT WHAT YOU HAVE READ IS TRUTH THEN ACT UPON IT. CUT OUT THE WORRYING AND BUILD UP THAT FEELING OF HAPPINESS AND CONTENTMENT – AS FROM NOW!'

Well, that is what I wrote in 1954, and I still understand that what I wrote then is basically true today.

However, some of you might pick me up on that word 'belief' and it does, I agree, need clarifying. I do *not* mean an unalterable conclusion. I do not mean, as I tried to explain in 'Do You Know

Over: 'Lesson of my life . . . that if one seeks one does indeed find.'

Limits exist
only in
your
mind.

What You Want' that one's *own* idea of what would make one happy should be paramount.

I mentioned 'successful' men as having 'belief in themselves' and Charles Forte said, 'You must believe in what you do to succeed.' Now I have known successful men and women who believed in themselves and in what they were doing but they have apparently failed. *Except* that they start again – and, if necessary, again and again. They *continue* to believe – or have confidence – in themselves. Perhaps it should be 'inside' themselves.

You remember that in an earlier chapter I spoke of a television programme in which I took part – the only one I have done in which I didn't say a word! – where I was demonstrating healing with myself and a patient linked up to two separate electro-encephalographs – brainwave measuring machines. And I said that true healers were said to show a strong 'Alpha' wave. This wave shows a relaxed, peaceful but confident state of mind. Others, besides healers, demonstrate a strong alpha wave. Athletes – those who are quietly confident for example. I bet you Steve Davis's alpha wave's a good 'un! Successful business men, too. Quietly determined people in *any* walk of life would show this wave, which is the wave predominant in meditation and relaxation when a person has slowed his thoughts and negative emotions.

It's a state of TRUST I'm talking about really. And one has to continue in a state of trust *no matter what happens.* No matter what goes apparently 'wrong' according to one's own judgment. Remaining with that state of trust is one of three factors which is going to bring about what I have referred to as 'happiness'. But 'happiness' is not really the right word because the root of that word 'hap' means 'luck'. And 'luck' has nothing to do with the peacefully joyful serenity I am talking about.

Hope, the second factor which I've mentioned, is defined in my dictionary – to which I've just referred – thus: 'To cherish a desire of good with expectation of obtaining it: to have confidence . . .' Hope strengthens the first factor.

But the third factor is the most important – and the most simple way I know in which to 'expand'. The problem is it is *so* simple that most people find great difficulty in attaining the degree of simplicity necessary to make it workable! *Because* most of us think of life as complicated and competitive. And life is what we think it is. What we believe it is. What we make it. According to our belief so it is to us. And if we change our ideas from fear and competitiveness to co-operation and an expansive outward-going loving kindness – no matter what others do – we, the individuals thinking in that way, benefit by gaining in confidence, understanding; oh! in so many ways which I cannot describe but which can be experienced. Bliss is how some describe it – or name it. 'An indescribable peace which nothing seems to move no matter what calamities occur,' is how someone attempted to define that state.

That peace is experienced when we cease to depend upon our limited human understanding. It is a wonderful peace which is not taken away when our plans go wrong. And it is a blissful peace which is far beyond the pleasures we experience when things do go our way!

May that peace of heart, mind and soul be known to you.

'Bye for now.

Also Available

WESTCOUNTRY MYSTERIES

Introduced by Colin Wilson. 45 photographs and drawings.

'The Westcountry isn't just a place of beauty . . . it is also a place of some curious mysteries . . . A team of authors have joined forces to re-examine and probe various yarns from the puzzling to the tragic . . . well-written and researched.'

James Belsey, *Bristol Evening Post*

DARTMOOR IN THE OLD DAYS

by James Mildren. 145 photographs.

James Mildren is an author who is at home in the wilderness of his Dartmoor.

'Lovers of Dartmoor will need no persuasion to obtain a copy. To anybody else, I suggest they give it a try. It may lead to a better understanding of why many people want Dartmoor to remain a wonderful wilderness.'

Keith Whitford, *The Western*

SEA STORIES OF DEVON

In this companion volume to *Sea Stories of Cornwall* nine Westcountry authors recall stirring events and people from Devon's sea past. Well illustrated with old and new photographs, it is introduced by best-selling novelist E. V. Thompson.

'The tales themselves are interesting and varied but the real strength of the book lies in the wealth of illustration, with photographs and pictures on practically every page.'

Jane Leigh, *Express & Echo*

UNKNOWN CORNWALL

by Michael Williams.

84 drawings and photographs, nearly all especially commissioned for this publication, portraying features of Cornwall rarely seen on the published page.

'. . . a treasure chest of rich jewels that will surprise many people who pride themselves on a thorough knowledge . . .'

Western Evening Herald

STRANGE SOMERSET STORIES

Introduced by David Foot with chapters by Ray Waddon, Jack Hurley, Lornie Leete-Hodge, Hilary Wreford, David Foot, Rosemary Clinch and Michael Williams.

'. . . a good collection of yarns about Somerset's eccentrics, weird legends and architectural follies . . .'

Dan Lees, *The Western Daily Press*

SUPERSTITION AND FOLKLORE
by Michael Williams. 45 photographs.
Romany reflections, old country customs, interviews with superstitious people, folklore from both Devon and Cornwall, omens and coincidences are all featured.
'. . . has all the ingredients of a mini-bestseller.'
Cornwall Courier

LEGENDS OF SOMERSET
by Sally Jones. 65 photographs and drawings.
Sally Jones travels across rich legendary landscapes. Words, drawings and photographs all combine to evoke a spirit of adventure.
'On the misty lands of the Somerset Plain – as Sally Jones makes clear – history, legend and fantasy are inextricably mixed.'
Dan Lees, *The Western Daily Press*

ECCENTRICS IN CORNWALL
by June Lander
With an introduction by Colin Wilson, June Lander has interviewed living people on the admission that they are eccentric.
'. . . fascinating details about the lifestyles . . . are bound to ensure another success for Bossiney.'
Cornwall Courier

VIEWS OF OLD PLYMOUTH
by Sarah Foot. 140 photographs.
Words and old pictures combine to recall Plymouth as it once was: a reminder of those great times past and of the spirit of the people of Plymouth.
'This is a lovely nostalgia-ridden book and one which no real Plymothian will want to be without.'
James Mildren, *The Western Morning News*

OCCULT IN THE WEST
by Michael Williams. Over 30 photographs.
Michael Williams follows his successful *Supernatural in Cornwall* with further interviews and investigations into the Occult – this time incorporating Devon. Ghosts and clairvoyancy, dreams and psychic painting, healing and hypnosis are only some of the facets of a fascinating story.
'. . . provides the doubters with much food for thought.'
Jean Kenzie, *Tavistock Gazette*

MY DEVON
Ten writers writing about their Devon: Hugh Caradon, Judy Chard, Andrew Cooper, Robin Davidson, Daniel Farson, Sarah Foot, Clive Gunnell, James Mildren, Mary and Hal Price.
'. . . ten writers' impressions of their favourite places . . . the personal approach warms and enlivens . . .'
Herald Express

CORNISH CHURCHES

by Joan Rendell. 60 photographs and drawings.

Here in her fifth title for Bossiney Joan Rendell explores many of Cornwall's lovely churches. Music and myths, art and architecture, personalities past and present are only some of the facets of her journey across the Cornish landscape.

'... an author who is well qualified to take us on a tour of Cornish Churches ... extremely readable.'

Cornish Guardian

STRANGE STORIES FROM DEVON

by Rosemary Anne Lauder and Michael Williams. 46 photographs.

Strange shapes and places—strange characters—the man they couldn't hang, and a Salcombe mystery, the Lynmouth disaster and a mysterious house are only some of the strange stories.

'A riveting read'. *The Plymouth Times*

'... well-written and carefully edited'.

Monica Wyatt, *Teignmouth Post & Gazette*

STRANGE HAPPENINGS IN CORNWALL

by Michael Williams. 35 photographs.

Strange shapes, and strange characters; healing and life after death; reincarnation and Spiritualism; murders and mysteries are only some of the contents in this fascinating book.

'... this eerie Cornish collection.'

David Foot, *Western Daily Press*

CORNISH MYSTERIES

by Michael Williams. 40 photographs.

Cornish Mysteries is a kind of jig-saw puzzle in words and pictures. The power of charming, mysterious shapes in the Cornish landscape, the baffling murder case of Mrs Hearn are just some fascinating ingredients.

'... superstitions, dreams, murder, Lyonesse, the legendary visit of the boy Jesus to Cornwall, and much else. Splendid, and sometimes eerie, chapters.'

The Methodist Recorder

LEGENDS OF CORNWALL

by Sally Jones. 60 photographs and drawings.

Brilliantly illustrated with photographs and vivid drawings of legendary characters. A journey through the legendary sites of Cornwall, beginning at the Tamar and ending at Land's End.

'Highly readable and beautifully romantic ...'

Desmond Lyons, *Cornwall Courier*

We shall be pleased to send you our catalogue giving full details of our growing list of titles for Devon, Cornwall and Somerset and forthcoming publications.

If you have difficulty in obtaining our titles, write direct to Bossiney Books, Land's End, St Teath, Bodmin, Cornwall.